Other titles in the HOW TO SAY IT® Series

How to Say It®

How to Say It® Best

How to Say It® at Work

How to Say It® for Couples

How to Say It® for Women

How to Say It® from the Heart

How to Say It® in Your Job Search

How to Say It® Online

How to Say It® to Teens

How to Say It® to Your Kids

How to Say It® with Your Voice

How Do You Spell Häagen-Dazs®?
    *The How to Say It® Book of Brands, Companies, Places,
    and Products Not Found in Your Dictionary*

How to Say It

STYLE GUIDE

ROSALIE MAGGIO

Prentice
Hall Press

Library of Congress Cataloging-in-Publication Data

Maggio, Rosalie.
  How to say it style guide / Rosalie Maggio.
       p.   cm.
  Includes index.
  ISBN 0-7352-0313-X (pbk.)
  1. English language—Style—Handbooks, manuals, etc.   2. English language—Grammar—Handbooks, manuals, etc.   3. English language—Usage—Handbooks, manuals, etc.   I. Title.

PE1460 .M264 2001
808'.042—dc21   2001053111

Copyright ©2002 by Rosalie Maggio

Printed in the United States of America

10 9 8 7 6 5 4 3 2 1

ISBN 0-7352-0313-X

Associate Publisher: *Ellen Schneid Coleman*
Production Editor: *Sharon L. Gonzalez*
Page Design/Layout: *Robyn Beckerman*

ATTENTION: CORPORATIONS AND SCHOOLS

Prentice Hall Press books are available at quantity discounts with bulk purchase for educational, business, or sales promotional use. For information, please write to: Prentice Hall Special Sales, 240 Frisch Court, Paramus, New Jersey 07652. Please supply: title of book, ISBN, quantity, how the book will be used, date needed.

Prentice Hall Press Paramus, NJ 07652

http://www.phpress.com

TO DAVID

Liz, Katie, Matt, Nora

Contents

Introduction

Have something to say and say it as clearly
as you can. That is the secret of style.

—Matthew Arnold

You have something to say. The *How to Say It® Style Guide* will help you say it clearly. With your ideas and this book, you can write an e-mail or an essay, a speech or a short story, a business report or a novel—all with style, grace, and confidence.

Part I provides you with the basics: eighteen brief guidelines for effective writing. Become familiar with these principles. Review them from time to time. Before long, you will be using them automatically.

Part II offers clear, brief, easy-to-find information about the most common writing problems. When you have a question, look up your key word. "Where do I put the apostrophe?" sends you to the entry **apostrophe**. To distinguish between *amount* and *number*, look up the word that comes first in the alphabet, and you'll find the entry **amount/number**. Because the competent writer uses a dictionary, any information that you can quickly find there is not duplicated here. For example, to determine the difference between *boat* and *ship* or between *principal* and *principle*, check your dictionary.

Part III alerts you to problem words. As you review these lists, you will develop an awareness of the most commonly misspelled, confused, long-winded, or unnecessary words and phrases.

This style guide is your assistant, not your boss. Your name goes on the report, article, letter, story, or proposal. Only your choices can produce the style that is uniquely yours.

I have made two assumptions about you, the reader: (1) you are bright, and (2) you are busy. With you in mind, I have organized this succinct and tidy collection of useful information to help you write correctly, fluently, and persuasively, both at work and at home. Here you'll find no more than you need to know for most writing tasks—and no less. I hope you find the content and the length of the *How to Say It® Style Guide*—as Goldilocks would have put it—"just right."

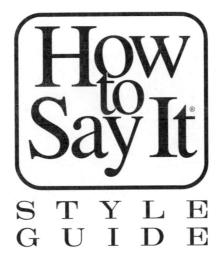

STYLE
GUIDE

The Eighteen Elements of Effective Writing

The beautiful part of writing is that you don't have to get it right the first time, unlike, say, a brain surgeon.

—ROBERT CORMIER

1. Use a dictionary. An online dictionary with spell-checking or a sturdy desk dictionary such as *The American Heritage Dictionary of the English Language*, 4th edition, will show you how to spell, hyphenate, capitalize, and accent words and phrases. If the dictionary gives two spellings for a word, use the first one. When it says the word you've looked up is a variant of another word, use the other word. If looking up words is a misery because you don't know how to spell them, buy a misspeller's dictionary (*Webster's New World Pocket Misspeller's Dictionary*, for example). When the word you want seems to hover just out of reach, a reverse dictionary such as *The Oxford Reverse Dictionary* will generally lead you from a related concept to the word you have in mind.

2. Think before you write. Sit back in your chair, put your feet on your desk (this is not only comfortable but will keep you from using pen or keyboard too soon), and think through what you want to say. Let your mind wander around your topic, but from time to time return to the center: Why are you writing this? What is your main idea or story? Keep thinking until you can formulate a one-sentence statement of your purpose in writing. Gail Godwin says, "Much of the activity we think of as writing is, actually, getting ready to write."

3. Organize your thoughts. In whatever way is most comfortable for you, jot down ideas, words, and phrases. Some people fill pages with words scrawled every which way and can make perfect sense of them. Others make lists or outlines. Think in terms of a beginning, middle, and end. How will you capture the reader's attention and introduce the purpose of your piece? What thought will you leave with the reader at the end? And how will you lay down a logical path from the beginning to your conclusion? Push yourself past your first, easy thoughts (Marilyn vos Savant says, "My thoughts are like waffles— the first few don't look too good") to the deeper thoughts that come from the rich subsoil. Once you have an idea of where you're going, fill in the outline by asking the classic questions: who, what, when, where, how, why. The reader needs to know the answers. You must supply them.

4. Gather information about your subject and check its accuracy. From looking up the address of someone to whom you're writing a letter to spending weeks in the library doing background research, pull together whatever you need to write correctly and completely. Depending on how you work, you can gather information and check facts after your brainstorming, during the writing, or while you're revising.

5. Start writing. Use conversational language and simple sentences. Don't worry about *how* you're saying it at this stage. *What* you're saying is more important. Get your ideas down on paper. Combine small units of thought (sentences) into larger ideas (paragraphs). Move the sentences and paragraphs around until they assume a logical relationship to each other.

6. Find the best word for your purpose. Every word in every sentence must pull its weight. Choose words that are concrete rather than abstract, precise rather than vague, familiar rather than unfamiliar, short rather than long, plain and simple rather than fancy and far-fetched—unless, of course, the unfamiliar, far-fetched word is precisely what you need. Choose sense-appealing picture nouns and active verbs rather than adjectives and adverbs. A thesaurus (J. I. Rodale's *The Synonym Finder* is excellent) will acquaint you with shades of meaning and may stimulate you to think of your material from new angles. However, beware of trading one almost-right word for another almost-right word. Replace empty words like *nice*, *beautiful*, *interesting*, *wonderful*, and *amazing* with specific descriptions of what makes the person or thing "wonderful." Read what you have written from beginning to end, while asking of all key words: "Is this the best word here?" You'll find helpful entries in this book under **adjectives, adverbs, nouns,** and **verbs.**

7. **Use dynamic verbs—and use them in the active voice.** When Sylvia Plath wrote that her love was "more athletic than a verb," she paid homage to the vigor and impact of a good verb. For more about verbs, see the entries **verbs** and **voice, active and passive.**

8. **Punctuate properly.** When in doubt, see the entries under **apostrophe, brackets, colon, comma, dash, ellipsis, exclamation point, hyphen, parentheses, period, question mark, quotation marks, semicolon,** and **slash.** The Web site *www.punctuation.org* has information and links to other sites. If you are intrigued by punctuation, grammar, and usage, invest in a grammar book (Anne Stilman's *Grammatically Correct* is excellent) and a usage guide (*The Oxford Dictionary of American Usage and Style* by Bryan A. Garner, for example). Professional writers use *The Chicago Manual of Style*, *The Associated Press Stylebook and Briefing on Media Law*, or other comprehensive usage and style books.

9. **Be clear.** Define the unfamiliar. Avoid jargon, slang, bureaucratese, euphemisms, high-flown language, and unnecessarily complicated phrases and clauses. Make sure the reader knows who, what, where, when, how, and why. Verify that pronouns refer to the correct person or thing. Watch for ambiguity, misplaced modifiers, and squinting constructions (a phrase that modifies either the words behind it or the words ahead of it, but one can't be sure which). Without patronizing readers, be certain they can grasp your main ideas; they shouldn't have to guess at them. Ask of every sentence: "Is the meaning clear?" If you are too close to your material, have someone else read it solely for clarity.

10. **Be specific.** Don't say "some" if there were fourteen, "cake" if they ate pineapple upside-down cake, or "chemical" if you mean hydrogen chloride. Be concrete rather than abstract ("she wept" instead of "she felt bad"). Instead of saying, "She was a miser," Mignon G. Eberhart described a character as being "tight as the paper on the wall." Concrete picture words and action verbs make your writing readable and memorable. You can tell by their evocative images which of the following sentence pairs have lasted for centuries: "Don't put all your hopes in just one thing" versus "Don't put all your eggs in one basket";

"Let's not fuss about our mistakes" versus "Let's not cry over spilled milk"; "You can be more successful with sweet talk than with harsh words" versus "You can catch more flies with honey than with vinegar."

11. Be concise. Unless you are aiming for a specific effect, keep sentences and paragraphs short. (Some writing authorities recommend an average sentence length of fifteen to twenty words.) Delete nonessential words, and whenever possible, replace several words with one precise word. Richard Peck says that you can cut ten words out of the tightest page you ever wrote. (See Part III for lists of unnecessary words and phrases.) How do you know what to delete? If you can remove a word, phrase, or sentence without loss of meaning, and if the tighter sentence or paragraph seems more powerful, you delete. Over the years, "Living well is the best revenge we can take on our enemies" has become "Living well is the best revenge." The succinct is usually more memorable.

12. Use parallel construction. In any series (of punctuation, names, verbs, adjectives, phrases, clauses, sentences, listings, ideas), be sure the elements are of the same type. For example, if you begin one paragraph with "First," begin the next paragraph with "Second," and the next with "Third." Nonparallel construction might use "First . . . , Secondly . . . , and (3)." In a list of instructions, parallel verbs would read: "to interview . . . to call . . . to meet with. . . ."

A nonparallel listing might begin with "to interview" but then talk about "calling the candidate" and end with "and, finally, you could meet with the staff." Examples of parallel structures: "Little children, little sorrows; big children, big sorrows"; "Pride rode out on horseback and came back on foot"; "Two's company, three's a crowd"; "In for a penny, in for a pound"; "Out of sight, out of mind"; "Be civil to all, sociable to many, familiar with few"; "Marriage halves our griefs, doubles our joys, and quadruples our expenses." See the entry on **parallel construction** for more on this essential of good writing.

13. **Be consistent.** Don't spell out "twelve" one time and use "12" the next. If you use (1), (2), and (3) as your style for one list, use it for all lists. If you are using present tense, don't switch to the past except for a good reason. When writing in the first person ("I think"), don't switch to second or third person ("you think"; "they think"). If you use a comma before *and* in a series anywhere in your piece ("Think much, speak little, and write less"), use it throughout.

14. **Vary your writing.** Mix long sentences with short sentences. Adjust word order so your sentences aren't all noun-verb-object. Move clauses, modifying phrases, and parenthetical expressions around to different places in the sentence. Don't seek variety for its own sake but for a more harmonious and meaningful whole. "Great oaks from little acorns grow" has more punch than "Great oaks grow from little acorns." "Curses, like chickens, come home to roost" is more rhythmic and memorable than "Curses come home to roost like chickens."

15. Elaborate. After your ideas are gathered and put into sentences and paragraphs, bring them to vivid life for the reader. Add definitions, examples, comparisons, contrasts, sensory details, analogies, similes, metaphors, and word pictures. To show an ineffective person, you might write, "If it were raining soup, he would be outside with a fork." Someone torn between courses of action might write, "I knew I couldn't ride two horses at the same time."

16. Be conscious of order and rhythm. To become an effective and elegant writer, study the way good writers play with word order and rhythm. A few tips:

1. Arrange your ideas or story from old to new, past to present, early to late; from general to specific (or vice versa); from the known to the unknown; from the simple to the complex. Build logically from one point to another.

2. Group similar words or phrases in threes. From our early encounters with the three bears, three billy goats gruff, three pigs, and three blind mice, through later acquaintance with such classics as "Hear no evil, see no evil, speak no evil," to the contemporary "Do not fold, spindle,

or mutilate," we find groups of three pleasing to our eyes and ears. In any group of three, there is usually a best way of organizing—from shortest to longest, from least to most intense. Juggle the three words or phrases to find the most appealing order.

3. Keep related sentence elements together, adjectives and adverbs close to the words they modify and clauses near the words they elaborate upon.

4. Subtle repetition, variants of a word, or opposites of a word provide satisfying echoes. Don't repeat words, phrases, or ideas needlessly, but consider the use of repetition when it can enhance your thoughts or your language.

5. Place the most important words in the sentence at the beginning or end. Compare these two versions: "A monkey remains a monkey though dressed in silk" and "A monkey dressed in silk is still a monkey." The second version delivers the punch line—the important word "monkey"—at the end.

17. **Keep your reader in mind.** Adjust your tone (will you be brisk, chatty, academic, formal, humorous?) and reading level (will you use sophisticated language, technical terms, or a fourth-grade vocabulary?) to your audience. Ideally, you should have some sense of how much readers know about your subject and what they would like to know about it. At key points ask yourself, "What would readers like to see here?" Sometimes they need a rest from tension, sometimes a bit of information to clarify what comes next, sometimes an unexpected development. Writers who forget about their readers often don't have many.

18. **Revise and rewrite.** Every good writer does it. Hemingway re-read and edited his books several hundred times. Dorothy Parker said, "I can't write five words but that I change seven," and Vladimir Nabokov claimed his pencils outlasted his erasers. You might

1. set your work aside for a few hours or a few days before proofreading it carefully;
2. read it through again, this time out loud so your ear can catch what your eye has missed;
3. ask someone with an analytical mind to read and evaluate it.

At this stage, check the following elements:

1. spelling, punctuation, grammar;
2. the orderly and clear progression of ideas, from beginning through middle to end, that conveys precisely what you mean to convey;
3. the right words in the right places with no unnecessary words or trite expressions (check the lists in Part III);

4. reader friendliness: Is the piece accessible and appealing? As you work on this draft, ask yourself: Is there a better word than this one? Is this phrase ambiguous? Is this word, sentence, or idea necessary? What would happen if I switched these sentences, paragraphs, or ideas? Is anything missing? Is that what I meant to say? Does it read smoothly, with transitions from one idea to the next?

Mary Heaton Vorse defined writing as "the art of applying the seat of the pants to the seat of the chair." Using these eighteen principles, you can apply pants to chair and achieve not only success (clear writing that does what you want it to do) but also happiness—in this case, discovering a new pleasure in the process of writing and a justified pride in your revitalized writing abilities.

Part II

A-Z
Style Guide

Think of writing as involving at least two drafts:
the down draft and the up draft. First you get it
down; then you fix it up. If you give yourself
permission to write an imperfect first draft,
you will find it easier to get started.

—STEPHEN WILBERS

a/an   Choosing between the indefinite articles is a problem only with words beginning with *h* or *u*. They take *a* when the *h* or *u* has a "heh" or a "you" sound ("Better a hen tomorrow than an egg today"; "in a uniform manner"). When the *h* or *u* has an open vowel sound, use *an* ("Have an umbrella ready before you get wet"; "an honorable discharge").

abbreviations   Avoid abbreviations, including the catchall *etc.*, except in the most casual writing. Replace *e.g.* with *for example* and *i.e.* with *that is.* In bibliographic references, the abbreviations *et al., op. cit.,* and *ibid.* are standard. Use two-letter state abbreviations on envelopes; they are acceptable inside on your letter. See also *acronyms.*

abstract/summary/synopsis   To summarize what you have written, list the essential points. Broaden them into sentences. Then reduce your sentences to the sparest prose, making sure verbs are in the same tense, structures are parallel, and the content of the longer work is clear. Depending on the length and complexity of the original work, an abstract, summary, or synopsis might range from one paragraph to two pages.

accent marks   Check your dictionary. Some words borrowed from other languages lose their accents in English (*naive, angstrom*); others retain them (*vis-à-vis, entrée*); still others are seen both ways (*café/cafe, cliché/cliche*).

acronyms   Except for acronyms certain to be familiar to your readers (SOS, CEO, CBS), spell out the terms on first use (Internal Revenue Service, Federal Bureau of Investigation, North Atlantic Treaty Organization, self-addressed stamped envelope). Later use the acronym (IRS, FBI, NATO, SASE). To put *a* or *an* before an acronym, determine how it would sound when spoken (an IRS form, an FBI agent, a NATO representative, an SASE).

adjectives "Nouns and verbs are almost pure metal; adjectives are cheaper ore" (Marie Gilchrist). Cheaper ore but still useful. The trick is to select adjectives with all the finickiness of a coin collector fallen on hard times. Strike out most of them, especially ones that have been overused or that do not evoke a picture for the reader (*great, fantastic, nice, beautiful, interesting, wonderful, amazing*).

Some adjectives cannot be compared. Something is perfect or it is not; it cannot, strictly speaking, be a more perfect union. In addition to *perfect*, adjectives that cannot be compared include *unique, preferable, absolute, whole, full,* and *fatal*.

adverbs   Adverbs (*slowly, greatly, magnificently*) modify verbs, adjectives, other adverbs, and sometimes nouns or pronouns. Omit them whenever you can by choosing a stronger verb (*dash* instead of *run quickly*). Some writers use the search function to hunt out and give a sharp look to their *-ly* adverbs.

Beware of replacing an adverb with an adjective: "Two can live cheaper than one" should be "Two can live more cheaply than one." He may be cheap, she may be cheap, but they live cheaply.

An old rule nixed splitting infinitives—that is, situating an adverb between *to* and the infinitive form of the verb: *to slowly make haste* is a split infinitive; *to make haste slowly* is not. Do whatever seems most graceful to you. Some people still consider a split infinitive an indication of poor language skills; however, most people understand that the rule was based on a Latin principle with no application to English. See also *real/really, very*.

almost   Don't use *most* when you mean *almost*: "Most any song will outlive a sermon in the memory" should be "Almost any song will outlive a sermon in the memory." Replace the awkward *almost never* with *rarely, hardly ever,* or *seldom.*

alphabetizing   To alphabetize words, phrases, lists, names, or other material, ignore spaces and punctuation between the terms and alphabetize letter by letter:

meat and potatoes	meat, frozen
meatballs	meat loaf
meat, carving	meat pies

Software programs sort (alphabetize) letter by letter. Word-by-word alphabetizing is less frequently seen:

meat and potatoes	meat pies
meat, carving	meat turnovers
meat, frozen	meatballs
meat loaf	

Names beginning with *Mc* are alphabetized letter by letter (Makeeba, McCartney, Mendelssohn). *St.* is alphabetized either as it appears (Sag Harbor, New York; Salem, Massachusetts; St. Paul, Minnesota) or as it would be if it were spelled out (Sag Harbor, New York; St. Paul, Minnesota; Salem, Massachusetts).

America/American   The people of some forty countries (those of North America, Central America and the

Caribbean, and South America) can correctly call themselves *Americans*. When possible, substitute a more precise term—for the country, *United States*, and for its inhabitants, *U.S. citizen/resident*. The use of *American* is ambiguous in such terms as *American history, American heroes*, and *American foreign policy*, and on the grounds of clarity alone should be replaced. Exceptions are terms like *Finnish Americans* and *Japanese Americans* since they are used only in the United States.

amount/number   Use *amount* for things that cannot be counted, *number* for things that can be counted. In the sentence, "We want bread and roses too," you could ask: How much bread? How many roses? They want an amount of bread and a number of roses. If it were "loaves of bread" (which can be counted), you could use "a number of loaves of bread."

ampersand (&)   Replace *&* with *and* except in titles of companies that use it (*AT&T*).

and/or   Use sparingly. Most readers either ignore it or come to a full stop in order to decipher its meaning.

antecedents   Antecedents are nouns that pronouns refer to; these nouns are found in the earlier part of the sentence or in a previous sentence. Be sure your reader knows which noun the pronoun is referring to: "If you don't feed the cats, you must feed the rats—and they know it!" Who knows it—the cats, the rats, or both?

When you need a pronoun for a collective noun (*company, family, agency, group, team*), generally use the singular: "Call it a clan, call it a network, call it a tribe, call it a family. Whatever you call it, whoever you are, you need one" (Jane Howard). However, if you want to emphasize the group as a collection of individuals, you may want the plural: "Family is just accident. . . . They don't mean to get on your nerves. They don't even mean to be your family, they just are" (Marsha Norman). The problem arises most often with such entities as *company* and *corporation*. You may correctly use either *it* or *they* to refer to them, as long as you are consistent.

any   Check the dictionary and the meaning of your sentence when using these: *any more/anymore; any place/anyplace; any time/anytime; any way/anyway*. The one-word terms are adverbs: "I can't do it anymore"; "He can live anyplace"; "She can do it anytime"; "He did it anyway." The two-word forms consist of adjective plus noun: "I can't eat any more"; "What may be done at any time will be done at no time"; "Any way you look at it, it's wrong." *Any one* and *anyone* are both pronouns, but *anyone* means a generalized "any person" ("Anyone who is always looking for mud generally finds it") and *any one* means a specific as-yet-unknown person ("Any one of you could have taken it"). Some of the other words that follow this adverb or noun-phrase pattern include *every day/everyday; one time/onetime; some time/sometime*. See also *compound words*.

apostrophe   The apostrophe has four functions: (1) to show possession: "Charles's aunt's cat's kittens' mittens are lost"; (2) to show that a letter is missing: "It's discouraging to hear words like can't, don't, shouldn't, oughtn't"; (3) to abbreviate years or decades: the '50s, the Gay '90s, the class of '65; (4) to clarify odd plurals: "She received all A's" is more easily read than "She received all As." See also *contractions, its/it's, plurals.*

as/like   *Like* and *as* connect two compared objects or actions. *Like* is always followed by a noun: "A mob is like a monster with many hands and no brains" (*like* is followed by the noun *monster*). *As* is followed by a noun and a verb: "When in Rome, do as the Romans do" (*as* is followed by the noun and verb *Romans do*).

   Correct: "He acts like a donkey standing between two bales of hay." *Like* is followed by the noun *donkey.* Correct: "He acts as if he is a donkey standing between two bales of hay." *As* is followed by the pronoun and verb *he is.*

   When you want to use *like*, first substitute *as* or *as if.* If either works, *like* is incorrect.

asterisk (*)   Use an asterisk to refer readers to a footnote (in material with only one or two footnotes). Most people can write for a lifetime without using one.

awhile/a while   In the phrase "Smile awhile," *awhile* is an adverb. In "Smile for a while," *a while* is an article and noun. *A while* almost always follows *for* ("For a while I didn't know if I was coming or going"). *Awhile* does not ("Why don't you sleep on it awhile?").

bad/badly   The adjective *bad* modifies nouns ("A bad excuse is better than none"). The adverb *badly* modifies verbs ("Reforms are most unpopular where they are most badly needed"). Problems arise with verbs like *feel, smell, taste,* and *look* when they take adjectives instead of adverbs: "Fish and visitors smell bad in three days." To "smell badly" indicates a problem with the sense of smell. The most common error is writing "feel badly." Correct: "I felt so bad about her accident"; "We feel bad that you can't come." "To feel badly" is hardly ever the right choice; we rarely complain about our sense of touch.

beginning, middle, and end   The beginning of a piece of writing must startle, mystify, interest, inform, or otherwise engage the reader. The middle places stepping-stones from one side of the river to the other; their purpose is not only to get the reader logically from beginning to end but to provide an interesting—and perhaps suspenseful—crossing. The end of your piece should be memorable, thought-provoking, inevitable, and satisfying.

between/among   Use *between* for two people or things ("There's many a slip between the cup and the lip"). Use *among* for three or more ("The great minds among us think alike"). Depending on whether there are two thieves or more than two, you'd write "honor between thieves" or "honor among thieves."

between you and me   Although "between you and I" is heard, it is always incorrect. Write instead "between you and me," "between Phaedra and me," "between the city council and me."

bi-/semi-   *Bi-* refers to something that occurs "every two" or "every other" (*biannual* means every other year; *bimonthly* means every other month; *biweekly* means every other week). *Semi-* means "twice a" (*semiannual* is twice a year; *semimonthly* is twice a month; *semiweekly* is twice a week). *Biennial,* thrown in for good measure, means "every second year" or "lasting for two years." Make it easy for your reader by using plain terms like *every other month, twice a week, every two years.*

biased language   When writing about people, your language must be accurate, precise, and respectful, and should not stereotype, exclude, or discriminate on the basis of sex, ethnicity, age, disability, socioeconomic class, sexual orientation, or religion. Stereotypes imply that members of a group (young mothers, rabbis, executives, teenagers, blue-collar workers, senior citizens, Asian Americans) are all alike. Write about people as individuals. In addition:

1. Follow the "people first" rule, which says we are people first and only secondarily people who have disabilities, people who are over sixty-five, people who are women, people who are Baptists, people who are black. Do you need to mention classifications such as sex, age, race, religion, economic class, or disability? Most often you don't.

2. Treat people in parallel fashion (if you mention one person's color, mention everybody's; if you say *female lawyer*, either say *male lawyer* or refer to both of them as *lawyers*).

3. Avoid sexist language such as using *he* when the person referred to could be a woman or a man ("He gives twice who gives quickly" can read "They give twice who give quickly"). Instead of the awkward *he and she*, replace or omit the pronoun, reword the sentence, use *you* or *we*, or recast the sentence in the plural. In addition, singular *they* ("to each their own") is considered acceptable and correct. It may sound awkward in some situations, so use your judgment. But always replace the false generic *he*. Also replace such words as *mankind, manpower, policeman*, and *mailman* with accurate, inclusive terms (for example, *mail carrier* is nonsexist, is used by carriers themselves, and is more descriptive than the vague word *mailman*).

4. Use *girl* for those under thirteen or even under fifteen; use *woman* in almost all cases instead of *lady*; avoid "feminine" endings such as *directress, adulteress, comedienne*, and *ancestress*.

5. A *handicap* is a feature of the environment that limits a person. For example, a building without ramps is a handicap to people with disabilities. Do not use *handicap* to refer to a disability. Avoid identifying the whole person by a part of the person; if Madeline has paraplegia, referring to her as "a paraplegic" identifies the whole Madeline by one part of her. People are not "confined to a wheelchair"; they "use a wheelchair." If your writing often touches on these

issues, refer to such resources as *The Handbook of Nonsexist Writing: For Writers, Editors and Speakers* by Casey Miller and Kate Swift; *Guidelines for Bias-Free Writing* by Marilyn Schwartz et al.; and *Talking About People: A Guide to Fair and Accurate Language* by Rosalie Maggio.

brackets   Save for emergencies. Brackets look officious, and sometimes the bracketed material contributes irrelevant or already known information: "All cats are grey [British spelling] in the dark."

Use brackets to insert clarifying material in a quotation. For example, Madame de Staël wrote, "One may almost call it [Italian] a language that talks of itself, and always seems more witty than its speakers."

Brackets are also used in or near a quotation when you italicize certain words for emphasis. You let your reader know that the italics were not in the original material by noting *[italics added]* or *[emphasis added]*.

Use brackets when you would like to put parentheses within parentheses but know you can't: "If you give them an inch, they'll take a mile (unless they're the neighbor's children, in which case they'll take a yard [thanks to Helen Castle for the witty addition])." Such uses are awkward and often need to be reworded.

can/may   *Can* conveys the idea of capability; *may* conveys the idea of possibility or permissibility: "You may lead a horse to water, but you can't make it drink" (it's possible and permissible to lead a horse to water, but you don't have the capability of making it drink).

capitalization   The dictionary will help with words that are always capitalized. In general, capitalize

1. proper names and places (Marie Marvingt, Cape Cod);

2. the first word of every sentence;

3. important words in a title;

4. names of months ("April showers bring May flowers") but not seasons (spring, summer, autumn, winter);

5. names of states (California) but not *state* as in *state of California*;

6. Mom, Dad, Uncle Matt, Grandpa Paul, Cousin Courtney; these titles act like names (you'd write "Dear Ramona" or "Dear Dad," not "Dear dad"). However, don't capitalize words like *mom* and *dad* when they are a generic label. None of the following should be capitalized: my mother, my teacher, her sister, her dentist, his brother-in-law, his boss.

Capitalize words that are parts of a name or title (Dean XX, Dr. XX, Community Health Agency, Department of Human Resources), but in general don't capitalize them when referred to later (the dean, the doctor, the agency, the department). Occasionally, though, you may want to capitalize the shortened reference for clarity. After mentioning "the Iowa Order of Odd Fellows" you might say, "Speaking on behalf of the Order leadership. . . ."

When in doubt about capitalization, you are often safer lowercasing words. The "up" style used to be popular: "It is eleven Year since I have seen my Figure in a Glass. The last Refflection I saw there was so disagreable, I resolv'd to spare my selfe such mortifications for the Future" (Lady Mary Wortley Montagu). Today the tendency is to use fewer capital letters. See also *titles*.

center   You cannot *center around* something; you *center on, center in*, or *center at*.

clichés   If it is something everyone says, don't say it. Clichés and platitudes have lost their sparkle—and often their meaning—through overuse. This book uses proverbs and sayings to demonstrate style issues. They are not fresh. They are not worthy of you. If you read it here (or anywhere else), don't use it in your writing.

colon   The colon precedes lists or long quotations, or it alerts the reader that something is coming ("There are three types of people: those who can count and those who can't"; "Crooks: it takes one to know one"). The colon is also used to

1. separate the main title from the subtitle (*Endangered Pleasures: In Defense of Naps, Bacon, Martinis, Profanity, and Other Indulgences* by Barbara Holland);

2. complete a formal business salutation ("Dear M.T. Brane:");

3. separate numbers in a ratio, and hours from minutes (1:2, 8:15);

4. complete statements beginning with *the following* or *as follows* ("The following are similes: dry as a bone, clean as a whistle, merry as a cricket").

Don't allow a colon to break up a sentence unnecessarily. For example, remove the colon in "It is difficult to hide: gold, love affairs, and a cough."

To decide between a colon and a semicolon, check to see if the material on either side of the punctuation is balanced. If it is, the sentence takes a semicolon. If the first part of the sentence seems to point toward the second, you probably want a colon ("Only one kind of worry is correct: to worry that you worry too much").

comma   Commas organize sentences logically, make them easier to read, and help deliver your meaning: "Poets and pigs, too, are appreciated only after their death"; "Poets, and pigs too, are appreciated only after their death." If you're not sure where the commas go, read the sentence aloud dramatically. The places where you pause may need commas. Use a comma

1. to separate the main elements of a sentence from each other ("Social tact is making your company feel at home, even though you wish they were");

2. after an introductory clause ("Once the camel gets its nose in the tent, its body will soon follow"; "If wishes were horses, beggars would ride"; "When the

cat is away, the mice will play") unless the introductory clause is short and clear ("Where there's smoke there's fire");

3. to set off an aside or a parenthetical element from the rest of the sentence ("A little knowledge, especially in medical matters, is a dangerous thing");

4. when two independent clauses are joined by a conjunction ("Everyone is crazy but me and thee, and sometimes I suspect thee a little") unless they are brief and straightforward ("Think today and speak tomorrow");

5. after the verb that introduces dialogue or a quotation (She said, "Forewarned is forearmed"; George Eliot wrote, "Breed is stronger than pasture");

6. to separate words that might otherwise be confusing ("In June, Johnson died"; "I'm fed up, up to here");

7. to separate city from state and the state from the rest of the sentence ("Boston, Massachusetts,") and to separate the date from the year and the year from the rest of the sentence ("By July 4, 1927, the coast was clear");

8. before and after "etc." ("Something old, something new, etc., didn't mean much to her");

9. to separate a series of items ("healthy, wealthy, and wise"). In a series, some people use a comma before *and*, and some prefer not to ("healthy, wealthy and wise"). Either is correct, although using the comma is a good choice because it clearly separates the items in the series.

Knowing where not to put a comma is also important. Do not use a comma anywhere between a noun and its verb (don't write "Too many cooks, spoil the broth"), although you may use two commas to set off a phrase between a noun and its verb ("Too many cooks, as we all know, spoil the broth"). In the same way, don't let a comma get between any elements that belong together. Look at your sentences in terms of groups of words. There should be no commas in the following sentences:

"At the door, of the rich, are many friends."

"He falls, on his back and breaks his nose."

"A fool, and his money, are soon parted."

"The ambitious bullfrog puffed, and puffed until it burst."

"What you don't know, won't hurt you."

comparative adjectives When comparing two items, use *more* or an *-er* ending: "It is more blessed to give than to receive"; "Blood is thicker than water." When comparing more than two, use *most* or the *-est* ending: "The most positive are often the most mistaken"; "One of the greatest labor-saving inventions of today is tomorrow."

compare to/compare with When comparing things that are dissimilar, use *compare to*. When comparing things that are similar, use *compare with*. "You can't really compare his bark to his bite" means that they are different. "When you compare his bark with his bite, there's not much to choose from" means that one is as bad as the other.

compose/comprise   The simplest way to use these two words correctly is to remember that *compose* takes *of* but *comprise* never does. *Is composed of* (a passive construction) has the same meaning as *comprises* (an active construction), and they both mean *is made up of*. The words "is comprised of" are always wrong. "It's raining cats and dogs" can be restated: "The rain is composed of cats and dogs"; "The rain comprises cats and dogs"; "The rain is made up of cats and dogs."

compound words   Do you want *back yard, back-yard,* or *backyard? Pick up, pick-up,* or *pickup? Run down, run-down,* or *rundown?* This will not be a welcome answer, but it depends—on whether you're using the term as a noun, adjective, or verb. The dictionary can help sort out the differences. In a pinch, read the sentence out loud and listen for tiny pauses. The goal is to find the form that makes the sense clear to your reader. See also *any, hyphens.*

conjunctions   Conjunctions that link two independent clauses (*although, and, because, but, for, if, nor, or, so, yet*) are usually preceded by a comma: "Love your neighbor, yet pull not down your hedge"; "Be a friend to thyself, and others will befriend thee." See also *as/like, run-on sentence.*

consistency   At the revision stage, check your writing for consistency:

> Do all phrases in a sentence, or sentences in a paragraph, belong to the same level and style of language?

> Is your tone the same throughout (not clipped in the beginning, meditative in the middle, and sarcastic at the end)?

> Are words that are capitalized in one place capitalized throughout the piece?

> Do you avoid switching needlessly from active to passive voice, from past to present tense, from third person to first person?

> In a series of nouns, have you allowed an adjective to creep in?

> Is your punctuation consistent throughout? For example, do you always use a serial comma ("Try, try, and try again") or never use a serial comma ("Try, try and try again")?

Perhaps no one but you will notice these details, but the reader—without knowing precisely why—will enjoy a sense of heightened satisfaction in reading prose that is consistent.

contractions   When a letter is left out in order to turn two words into one, an apostrophe takes its place: *don't, can't, o'clock, something's cooking, there's one born every* *minute, the fat's in the fire.* Contractions confer a degree of informality on the written word. The common verb contractions (*don't, won't, shouldn't*) are acceptable in almost all situations. Except for *it's*, contractions of nouns and verbs (*there's one, the customer's always right*) are generally too casual for standard writing. The degree of informality, and thus your use of contractions, will depend on your material and on your audience. See also *apostrophe, its/it's.*

convince/persuade   Although this distinction is losing some ground in popular usage, good writers still observe it. *Persuade* involves action and is generally found with *to* ("He persuaded me to jump from the frying pan into the fire"). *Convince* involves thought and is found with *that* or *of* but never with *to* ("She convinced me that curiosity had killed our cat").

couldn't care less   Correct. "I could care less" makes no sense as it is commonly used.

couple   "Always have a couple of strings to your bow"; "a couple strings" (without the *of*) is incorrect. *Couple* can refer to two things or, used casually, to a few or several things.

dash   Once the dash habit takes hold, dashes proliferate on the page, giving the material a—well—slapdash quality. Effectively used, however, dashes clarify and civilize many sentences. "They swallowed the bait, hook, line, and sinker" becomes unambiguous with a dash: "They swallowed the bait—hook, line, and sinker." Sometimes the dash adds emphasis: "Don't trust people too much—or too little." When using the dash to mark off a clause or explanatory expression, remember the second dash: "Cash—plenty of it—is the lifeblood of the nation."

different from/different than   *Different from* is almost always the correct choice ("A bird in the hand is different from two in the bush"). Only rarely will you use *different than*: "Making a silk purse out of a sow's ear turned out to be different than he'd expected."

double negative   The old proverb uses multiple negatives to emphasize its point: "Nobody don't never get nothing for nothing, nowhere, no time, nohow." Double negatives are a problem when they make your sentence say the opposite of what you intended: "The game isn't hardly worth the candle"; "Barking dogs don't hardly ever bite." Occasionally, a double negative used properly can emphasize a point: "She couldn't not make bricks when she was given straw."

each other/one another   Two people take *each other* for better or worse; the wedding party gives *one another* hugs after the ceremony because the wedding party consists of three or more people. Because *each other* and *one another* are already plural constructions, add *'s* for plural possessive: they paid for *each other's* rings; the congregation shook *one another's* hands.

either/or; neither/nor   These pairs work together; *either/nor* and *neither/or* are unacceptable.

ellipsis   An ellipsis has three purposes:

1. It indicates that some quoted material is missing: "Harry is walking with a cane these days. . . . What necessitated the cane was the fact of Young Cat scampering among Harry's ankles at a moment when Harry happened to be walking among them himself" (Margaret Halsey).

2. It shows hesitation or trailing off in speech ("A penny for your thoughts . . .").

3. It lends extra significance to parts of a sentence: "They are the most painful tears in the world . . . the tears of the aged . . . for they come from dried beds where the emotions have long burned low" (Bess Streeter Aldrich).

To quote from part of a longer passage, you do not need to use an ellipsis at the beginning or at the end of the sentence, but you must use it in the middle. When people read quotations, they assume that something went before and that something came after the lines you're citing. Instead of ". . . making a decision to write was a lot like deciding to jump into a frozen lake," write: "Making a decision to write was a lot like deciding to jump into a frozen lake" (Maya Angelou).

When an ellipsis comes at the end of a sentence, add a fourth dot for the period that would normally be there. If the omitted material comes after the period, so does the ellipsis: "I like not only to be loved, but also to be told that I am loved. . . . I shall take leave to tell you that you are very dear" (George Eliot). If the omitted material comes before the period, so does the ellipsis: "We didn't talk so much about happiness in my day. When it came, we were grateful for it . . . . We may have been all wrong in our ideas, but we were brought up to think other things more important than happiness" (Ellen Glasgow).

Type an ellipsis by using one space, three periods, and one space ("A good example ... is the best sermon") or with three spaced periods ("A good example . . . is the best sermon"), but be consistent whichever you choose.

etc./et cetera   Avoid this catchall term, which gives a careless look to a sentence. When you use it, never precede it with *such as*. *Etc.* means "and everything else" and *such as* says "here are a few examples." You can't have both "a few examples" and "everything else."

exclamation point   Lewis Thomas explains why exclamation points are irritating: "Look! they say, look at what I just said! How amazing is my thought! It is like being forced to watch someone else's small child jumping up and down crazily in the center of the living room shouting to attract attention. If a sentence really has something of importance to say, something quite remarkable, it doesn't need a mark to point it out. And if it is really, after all, a banal sentence needing more zing, the exclamation point simply emphasizes its banality!" Exclamation points give your writing a manic look, like people laughing at their own jokes. At first it will grieve you to remove them; by and by you will be pleased to find you can get along nicely without them. Restrict their use to dialogue ("Open, Sesame!") or to the rare occasion when you judge one to be necessary.

farther/further   Reserve *farther* for physical distance ("I live farther from the ocean now") and *further* for figurative distance ("I'll give it further thought").

fewer/less   Use *fewer* for numbers, for anything that can be counted, and use *less* for amounts, for anything that cannot be counted: "We're having less trouble with the power supply this year and fewer problems with the new software"; "I'm writing less autobiographical material and fewer poems this year." The problem most frequently occurs when *less* is used instead of the correct *fewer*.

film titles   *See titles.*

first/firstly   Use first, second, third, etc., rather than firstly, secondly, thirdly.

flammable/inflammable   Confusingly enough, these words mean the same thing. Use *flammable*; its meaning is more obvious.

foreign words/phrases   Words borrowed from other languages that have become familiar to us appear in regular type: "He had no idea he'd committed a faux pas"; "She worked on a kibbutz for six years." Unfamiliar expressions are often unnecessary and usually annoying. When you must use one, italicize it: "His answer to everything was an indecisive *più o meno*." In some cases, explain it: "She asked to be buried where she had lived, next to the *sindhu* (river)."

good/well   The adjective *good* modifies nouns ("Good things come in small packages"). The adverb *well* modifies verbs ("What is worth doing is worth doing well"), but it is also an adjective meaning healthy ("She is well again") or in a satisfactory condition ("All is well"). When describing an action, use *well*: "Dudley works well by himself." When writing about a thing, use *good*: "We are remembered by our good deeds, not by our good intentions." Verbs such as *smell, taste*, and *look* take adjectives: "Peach ice cream smells good, tastes good, and looks good."

hardly   Check any sentence with *hardly* to be sure you don't have another negative near it. Incorrect: "The right hand doesn't hardly know what the left hand is doing."

however   The placement of *however* will be a matter for your eye and ear. Some writers object to using it at the beginning of a sentence. However, if you use it that way, follow it with a comma to avoid confusion with its other use ("However you look at it, this situation is a horse of a different color").

Some writers think the best place for it is inside a sentence, set off by commas ("A friend in need, however, is a friend indeed").

When *however* introduces the second of two independent thoughts, it needs a semicolon before it: "Moderate riches will carry you; however, if you have more, you must carry them."

hyphen   When in doubt, check the dictionary for words that take a hyphen (*anti-inflammatory, front-runner, off-putting, pro-choice*). If your term isn't listed in the dictionary as one word or as a hyphenated word, it is written as two words.

Add hyphens to link words into an easy-to-read thought group when the reader might not quickly make the association ("It is better to be a has-been than a never-was") or when the word could be ambiguous ("recreation" and "re-creation").

Hyphenate two-word adjectives that precede nouns: "wild-goose chase," "rose-colored glasses," "old-time religion." Do not, however, hyphenate them when they follow the noun ("well-behaved children" but "the children were well behaved"). And do not hyphenate two-word modifiers that include *-ly* adverbs: "newly appointed director"; "poorly constructed home." (The *-ly* words don't need to be hyphenated because the reader expects them to modify whatever follows.) When in doubt, remember that the chief use of the hyphen is to make it easy for your reader to grasp your material quickly. If a hyphen will help your reader, use it. See also *compound words*.

imply/infer   In the movie *D.O.A.*, Dennis Quaid, playing an English professor, explains patronizingly, "When I say something, that's implying. How you take it is inferring." *Imply* means to suggest something; *infer* means to conclude, surmise, or deduce something from what another person said.

indenting   Set the first word of each paragraph five to ten spaces from the left margin (whatever looks good to you). If you prefer not to indent, leave a line of space between paragraphs to signal the break. The purpose of indenting is to make it easy for the reader. If you have lists, indent them. If you insert a lengthy quotation, set it off from the rest of the text by indenting it (in this case, do not use quotations marks). Example: In *Northanger Abbey* (1818), Jane Austen shows what she thinks of the word *nice*:

> This is a very nice day; and we are taking a
> very nice walk; and you are two very nice
> young ladies. Oh! it is a very nice word,
> indeed! it does for everything.

If your material is to be published, a production editor will either tell you beforehand about any special indenting or will take care of it during the editing and printing process.

initials   See *acronyms, spacing*.

italics Use italics for

1. titles of books, movies, plays, operas, magazines, newspapers, paintings, drawings, and statues, and names of ships, planes, space vehicles, and trains;

2. unfamiliar foreign words;

3. words with special significance or words used as words (see *words/letters used as words/letters*);

4. words in a quotation that you want to call to the reader's attention. In this last case, put *[italics added]*, *[emphasis added]*, or *[italics mine]* after the italicized words, as is done in this quotation from Harriet Martineau:

   Authorship has never been with me a matter of choice. I have not done it for amusement, or for money, or for fame, or for any reason but *because I could not help it* [italics added]

Some writers italicize words in an attempt to lend emphasis, significance, and excitement to their words. Don't do this; italics cannot replace the hard work of good writing. See also *quotation marks, titles*.

its/it's One of the most common errors is using one of these small words when the other one is called for. Correct: "It's a mistake to judge a book by its cover." If you cannot write *it is* in place of your word, use *its*—no apostrophe. If this is one of your weak spots, write only *it is* or *its* until you are comfortable with the difference.

jargon   Use jargon judiciously. When writing for those in your field, it can reveal you as a knowledgeable insider. When communicating with an audience outside your field, it is irritating and confusing.

lay/lie   The verb *lay* (with past tense *laid*, past participle *laid*, and present participle *laying*) takes an object: "Don't kill the goose that lays the golden eggs"; "They killed the goose that laid the golden eggs"; "They killed the goose that was laying the golden eggs." The verb *lie* (with past tense *lay*, past participle *lain*, and present participle *lying*) does not take an object: "Let sleeping dogs lie"; "We let the sleeping dogs lay"; "The sleeping dogs had lain there for hours"; "The sleeping dogs were lying there peacefully."

like   See *as/like*.

lists   Arrange lists logically from top to bottom in order of importance, chronology, sequence, usefulness, size, or some other measure. Indent the entire list and leave an extra line of space above and below it. Checklist for lists:

1. Each item is necessary and unique.

2. Each item is constructed parallel to the other items (all nouns or all verbs, all capitalized or all not capitalized, each ending with the same punctuation or no punctuation).

3. Each item is set off by a bullet, number, or icon to make it stand out from the others.

literally   "Her hair literally stood on end." Probably not. *Literally* is so seldom used correctly that if you don't have a good grasp of its meaning, you may as well make up your mind never to use it. What is usually meant is: "She felt that her hair was standing on end." Substitute the word *actually* for *literally*; if it works, *literally* is correct: "I literally/actually ran into her on the street; her leg is still in a cast."

metaphors   A metaphor substitutes one thing for another or says one thing *is* another. The implicit comparison makes the second thing more vivid for the reader: "A good conscience is a soft pillow." (Conscience = pillow.)

"Habits are at first cobwebs and at last cables." Habits, of course, are neither cobwebs nor cables, but the metaphor makes us see habits in a new way.

Elegant, effective metaphors produce some of the strongest, most memorable writing. Bad metaphors, however, are worse than none. Don't use outworn metaphors ("A rolling stone, he gathered no moss"); don't daze the reader with too many of them; be careful that metaphors don't muddy rather than sharpen the picture ("Are you still driving that old coffeepot?"); and watch for mixed metaphors ("The iron hand in the velvet glove was as soft as silk"). See also *similes*.

misplaced modifiers   Also called dangling modifiers, these words and phrases are tucked into a sentence in such a way that the reader doesn't know what they modify: "Buttered on both sides, he ate his daily bread with greed and gratitude." What is buttered on both sides?

Surely not "he," which the phrase modifies. When whatever is being modified is unknown or unclear, you have a misplaced modifier. Move the modifying phrase closer to what it modifies.

A squinting modifier is one that might be modifying something behind it or something ahead of it; nobody knows.

At the revision stage, study your sentences in terms of word groups and thoughts to make sure readers know what goes with what.

more/most important/importantly   As introductory phrases, *more* or *most important* and *more* or *most importantly* are both correct: "More importantly, you ungrateful wretch, never look a gift horse in the mouth"; "Most important, loose lips sink ships."

negative/positive   Be aware of whether you are phrasing sentences in the negative ("Don't walk on the grass") or in the positive ("Please walk on the sidewalk"). Negative constructions are sometimes necessary, but positive sentences are recommended for most situations.

noun-verb agreement   Nouns and verbs must "agree" with each other: if the noun is singular, the verb is singular, and if the noun is plural, so is the verb. However, this reasonable arrangement is not as simple as it looks:

1. The most common problem arises when words come between the noun and the verb: "An apple a day (if,

of course, it's been organically grown and flown fresh from the garden to your door within days) keeps the doctor away." *Apple* is obviously a singular noun, but by the time one wades through the intervening words, and perhaps becomes distracted by the plural *days* next to the verb, it is easy to forget to make *keeps* singular. When proofreading your writing, find each noun and verb, especially in long sentences, and put them together to see if they agree.

2. The noun and verb agree even when what follows is a different number: "The problem here is wild oats." *Problem* and *is* are singular, even though *wild oats* is plural.

3. *A number of* is always treated as plural ("A number of us are living in a fool's paradise"); *the number of* is always treated as singular ("The number of new brooms sweeping clean after every election is astonishing").

4. To decide whether two or more nouns (a compound subject) take a singular or plural verb, determine whether they act as one or as more than one. In "To forgive and to forget is not easy," the two subjects act as one idea. In "Forgive and forget are the most difficult commands in the language," *forgive* and *forget* count as two things; therefore, they take a plural verb, *are*.

5. When the compound subject is joined by *or*, the verb may be singular or plural: "an apple or a banana is"; "apples or oranges are"; "an apple or two oranges are"; "two oranges or an apple is." When both are singular, the verb is singular; when both are plural, the verb is plural;

when one is singular and one is plural, whichever one is nearest the verb governs the verb's number.

6. Some nouns that look plural take a singular verb: "This series of books is being judged by its covers."

7. When a plural noun is preceded by *every one of* or a similar construction, the verb is always singular: "If you pull one pig by the tail, every one of the others squeals"; "Every one of the donkeys thinks its own pack heaviest."

8. *None is* a problem, or *none are* a problem, depending on the meaning. More often than not, *none* is considered a plural. Use *none is* when you mean *none of it is*: "None of their charity begins at home." Use *none are* when you mean *none of them are*: "When I make an omelet, none of the eggs are broken."

9. Don't use *there's* when you mean *there are* ("There are pins and needles spilled on the carpet" rather than "There's pins and needles spilled on the carpet").

10. *Data*, *media*, and *criteria* are all plural and thus should take plural verbs. However, *data* and *media* are more and more being used with singular verbs ("The data from the last run is astonishing"; "The media is wrong on this one"). Thus far, *criteria* and its singular form *criterion* seem to be used correctly.

number is/number are   *The number* takes a singular verb: "The number of new tricks this dog can learn is shrinking." *A number* takes a plural verb: "A number of pearls are being cast before swine."

numbers   You may decide which numbers to write out and which to write as numerals, but be consistent. Many people write out numbers one through nine ("A stitch in time saves nine") and use Arabic numerals for numbers over nine ("They were 32 birds of a feather flocking together"). Others write out all numbers under 100.

Express approximate numbers in words (*some three hundred people*).

Fractions generally do not stand alone (¼) but are accompanied by a number (3¼). Exceptions include scientific writing and recipes. Write out fractions when they stand alone (*one-fourth*) or when they begin a sentence: "Two-and-one-half minutes to go!" Use hyphens when fractions are expressed in words. The preposition *of* is usually unnecessary with the word *half*: "Half a loaf is better than none."

Styles vary for percentages. However, unless your writing is extremely formal (in which case you write *forty-nine percent* or sometimes *49 percent*), set percentages in figures (*49%*) for ease of reading.

A sum of money is *$100*, not *$100.00* and not *$100 dollars*.

okay/OK/O.K.   All three forms are correct, although *OK* and *O.K.* are more appropriate for informal writing and dialogue than for more formal writing.

only/not only   Place these terms immediately before the word they modify. For example, see how the meaning of the following sentence changes when you position *only* as the first word, the second word, and so forth: "Nadia bearded the lion in its den."

outline   The most common system for outlining includes, in descending order of importance, the following letters and numbers: I., II., III., etc.; A., B., C., etc.; 1., 2., 3., etc.; a., b., c., etc.; i., ii., iii., etc. An outline of an article on dogs might look like this:

I.   Origin and History
II.   Behavior
    A.   Territory and range
    B.   Group behavior
        1. in dogs
        2. in wolves
            a.   Simpson study
            b.   Lerner-Wilson study
                i.   reproduced data
                ii.   unreproduced data
                iii. disputed data

paragraph   For most writing, short paragraphs work best. Develop a single idea in each paragraph, working either from your broadest point (topic sentence) to the details that support it, or beginning with details that lead the reader to the big picture—your final, topic sentence. The last sentence of every paragraph should allow you to build on it to begin the next paragraph.

parallel construction Structure your words and ideas so that they balance each other. The sentence "We invited Jack, one of those people born with a silver spoon in his mouth, and Bob" lacks parallel structure.

The words *and* and *or* and sometimes a comma or semicolon act like the fulcrum in a seesaw; on either side of it the words should have equal weight.

In the sentence "Children have more need of models than of critics," *of models* and *of critics* are parallel structures. The meaning changes when they are no longer parallel: "Children have more need of models than critics" implies that children need models more than critics do.

Contrast parallel and nonparallel constructions:

"Pamela Hansford and Richard Shreve" (not "Mrs. Pamela Hansford and Richard Shreve");

"college men and college women" (not "college men and college girls");

"A clock that stands still is better than one that goes wrong" (not "A clock that stands still is better than one going wrong");

"If they deceive me once, shame on them; if they deceive me twice, shame on me" (not "If they deceive me once, shame on them; if they deceive me twice, it will be my own fault").

See also *consistency*.

parentheses Put offhand comments and asides in parentheses: "Creditors (at least the ones I know) have better memories than debtors." Parenthetical remarks are separate from the main flow of the sentence and can be removed without greatly changing the meaning of the sentence. If you were speaking, you would pause and alter your voice slightly to deliver a parenthetical remark.

When a complete sentence is in parentheses, capitalize and punctuate it as you would any independent sentence, placing all punctuation inside the parentheses: (Not they who have little, but they who wish for more, are poor.)

Parenthetical material inside a sentence can be an incomplete thought or a complete sentence. Lowercase the first word and omit the period: "Wit is the salt (and sometimes the pepper) of conversation." "She didn't act as though she cared (my father always said that actions spoke louder than words)."

Punctuate the rest of the sentence exactly as you would if the parenthetical material wasn't there: "When one door shuts (or seems to shut), another opens."

There should be no punctuation before a parenthetical expression. The comma after *going* is wrong: "going, (but six did)." The colon after *following* is also wrong: "the following: (except for the first two)."

At the proofreading stage, check to see that each parenthesis has a mate; it's easy to forget the second one.

When do you set off a phrase with commas and when with parentheses? Use commas when the material is closely related to the material in the sentence: "A thief knows a thief, as a wolf knows a wolf, so the Kid recognized Duval at once." Parentheses alert the reader to material of secondary importance: "Misfortunes never came singly (at least not in her experience)."

people/persons Don't use *persons*; it's one person, two or more people.

period The period functions as a stop sign at the end of a sentence. Or sentence fragment. It also follows every abbrev. When a sentence ends in an abbreviation, don't add a second period. In the same way, a period is not needed after a question mark or an exclamation point.

Periods (or dots) serve as decimal points (6.25%), as ellipsis (see *ellipsis*), and as organizers after numbers in a list (1. Foxes; 2. Sheep; 3. Cabbages, etc.). Note that *etc.* needed its own period, but because it was inside parentheses, the sentence needed a period of its own. See also *parentheses, quotation marks, spacing.*

permission See *quotations.*

plurals A good dictionary gives plurals of words that form them irregularly (that is, in some way other than by adding an *s* or *es*):

crisis/crises	leaf/leaves
criterion/criteria	moose/moose
family/families	potato/potatoes

Plurals of numbers and acronyms take an *s*:

the 1980s, CEOs, four 10s, the '30s, CODs

Add an apostrophe to plurals when necessary for clarity: "What does it mean if people never use I's in their letters?") To make a proper noun plural, add *s* (*all my Novembers, the Smiths, both Janets were there*) or *es* (*the Nashes, the Thomases in this family*). Do not put an apostrophe in a name when it is simply plural; too many people already think of themselves incorrectly as the Olmstead's or the Dickinson's.

In a compound noun, generally add the plural to the main part of the term (*brothers-in-law, passersby*). When a word is italicized, add the *s* or *es* in regular type ("I dreamed there was a fleet of *Titanic*s"). See also *possessives*.

plus   Don't use *plus* to introduce an independent clause: "You're counting your chickens before they're hatched, plus, you don't have any eggs." Generally, *and* will do the job nicely.

poetry   When quoting two or more lines of poetry or verse in the text, use a slash to show where the lines end: "I am dark but fair, / Black but fair" (Alice Meynell). Keep all punctuation and capitalization as it is in the original. Before quoting poetry in writing to be published, inform yourself of the permissions issues involved.

possessives   To show possession by a singular noun, add *'s*: "Cutting off a mule's ears won't make it a horse." "Anger is a stone cast at a wasp's nest."

To show possession by a plural noun, add *s'*: "We can always bear our neighbors' misfortunes." "Fools' names, like fools' faces, are often seen in public places." When a plural is formed by adding *es*, the apostrophe still goes after the *s*: "One eye-witness's report is better than ten ear-witnesses' reports."

Children's, men's, and *women's* are the correct plural possessives, using *'s* instead of the usual *s'* because the base words are already in the plural.

Treat names as you would other nouns: in "John Brown's Body," there is only one person, so you add *'s*. In "The Browns' house has a wolf at the door," *Browns* is plural, so you add an apostrophe to the *s*.

Nonphysical entities also show possession, as in *six years' worth, a month's leave, a day's notice, four hours' work.*

prepositions, ending a sentence with The Latin origins of this "rule" are irrelevant today; if you need to end a sentence with a preposition, go ahead. However, the last word in a sentence should generally be strong or significant—and prepositions are rarely either. The goal is a well-written sentence, wherever the preposition works best.

pronouns Pronouns generally behave themselves. One recurring error is heard in the ubiquitous and never-correct "between you and I." When two or more pronouns are the object of a verb or of a prepositional phrase, all the pronouns are in the objective case:

> "Too many cooks spoiled the broth for Sandy and me."

> "He always played second fiddle to Kit and me."

> "You may need to handle her and me with kid gloves."

The error involves substituting *I* for *me*. If *me* sounds awkward to your ears, which it may sometimes, replace noun and pronoun or pronoun and pronoun with *us*. A simple test is to remove the other person and see if you would say *for I* or *for me*, or *to I* or *to me*.

The other common pronoun problem is using *he* when you mean *he and she* or when you refer to someone who could be a man or a woman (for example, *the consumer . . . he*). Because *she and he* is awkward to read and quickly becomes tiresome, avoid it when possible. Instead, make your sentence plural; change the pronoun to first or second person; omit the pronoun altogether; reword the phrase; or, as a last resort, recast in the passive voice. A good solution, which most influential dictionaries and language organizations now approve, is the indefinite *they*: "Nobody knows what another person is thinking. They may imagine they do, but they are nearly always wrong" (Agatha Christie). See also *between/among, between you and me, -self, that, that/which, who/whom/whoever/whomever, who's/whose*.

question mark   A direct question ("Did you get up on the wrong side of the bed?") always ends in a question mark.

Indirect questions do not: "She asked me if an apple a day really keeps the doctor away." She asked a direct question, but now that someone else is relaying it, it's no longer direct.

Rhetorical questions do not take question marks either: "Well, how do you like that!"

To merit a question mark, a question must be asked directly of another person and an answer must be expected.

The only punctuation mark that can follow a question mark is a quotation mark, a parenthesis, or a bracket. In the following sentence, no comma is used before the ending quotation mark: "Did you pull the wool over their eyes?" she asked.

quotation marks   Use quotation marks to demonstrate that you are quoting from other material; to indicate the titles of poems, articles, essays, short stories, TV series, and song titles; and to set off dialogue: The ant said to the elephant, "Let's be sports and not step on each other."

All commas and periods—and all exclamation points and question marks that belong to the quotation—go inside the quotation marks: "What?" "Egads!" "I won't," he said. Common sense will indicate when a question mark or exclamation point goes outside the ending quotation mark, for example, when the punctuation in no way belongs to the quoted text: When did he first say "I love you"?

Colons and semicolons that are not part of the quoted material always go outside the ending quotation mark: One proverb says, "Company in misery makes it light"; another says, "Misery loves company."

Quotation marks also set off words used as words (see *words/letters used as words/letters*) or words that need to be set apart from the rest of the sentence: "Almost" never killed a fly.

Use either quotation marks or *so-called*, but not both, when casting doubt on something: Jane Goodall said that every individual can make a difference; "if we continue to leave decision making to the so-called decision makers, things will never change." She could also have written "leave decision making to the 'decision makers.'"

To link words into a phrase, use either quotation marks ("Almost made it" never made the grade) or hyphens (Almost-made-it never made the grade), but not both.

In dialogue, begin a new paragraph each time the speaker changes. When the same speaker starts a new paragraph, do not place a quotation mark at the end of the previous paragraph, but do place a quotation mark at the beginning of the new paragraph. There is no final quotation mark until that character has stopped speaking altogether.

Don't use quotation marks around a character's thoughts.

When you have a quotation within a quotation, use single quotation marks for the internal quote: "The two most beautiful words in the English language are 'check enclosed,'" wrote Dorothy Parker. See also *italics, titles*.

quotations   When you are quoting someone's words precisely, use quotation marks and give the source. If it is a brief quotation, run it into the text: Will Rogers said, "America has the best politicians money can buy." Longer quotations can be set off as follows:

> Oh! this continually accumulating debt of cor-
> respondence! It grows while we sleep, and
> recurs as fast as we can pay it off. . . . I know no
> greater delight than to receive letters; but the
> replying to them is a grievous tax upon my neg-
> ligent nature. I sometimes think one of the
> greatest blessings we shall enjoy in heaven will
> be to receive letters by every post and never be
> obliged to reply to them.
>
> —Washington Irving, in Pierre M. Irving, ed.,
> *The Life and Letters of Washington Irving,*
> vol. 2 (London: Richard Bentley, 1862)

When quotations are run into the text, use quotations marks; when they are set off and indented, do not
use them. When you are quoting someone indirectly, do
not use quotation marks but give the source: Henri
Frédéric Amiel used to say that the great art of teaching
was all in knowing how to make suggestions.

You can quote part of a sentence: An anonymous
wag once claimed it was easy to meet expenses:
"Everywhere we go, there they are."

Double-check every word and punctuation mark
when quoting someone else's words in a work to be published; quotations must be correct. And most often you
must seek permission to use excerpts from published
works. See also *quotation marks, [sic], words/letters used as
words/letters.*

real/really Use *real* as an adjective ("real diamonds";
"real wheatberries") and *really* as an adverb ("that really

takes the cake"; "it really rained on their parade"). Beware of using *real*, the adjective form, to modify another adjective instead of using *really*, the adverb form. Incorrect: "A real heavy purse makes a real light heart"; "The used key is always real bright." Correct: "A really heavy purse makes a really light heart"; "The used key is always really bright."

reason   The correct form is *the reason . . . is that*, not *the reason . . . is because*. (*The reason why* is acceptable, although somewhat awkward.)

redundancies   Check to see that you aren't saying the same thing in different ways: "I believe that two heads are better than one. In addition, four eyes see more than two. What I'm saying is the more the merrier."

From small redundancies like "let's us" (which actually says "let us us") to the thinly disguised rehashing of the same thoughts throughout an essay, repeating yourself without a good stylistic or pedagogic reason for doing so will weary your reader.

Acronyms often contain a word that tends to get tacked on (it's *ATM*, not *ATM machine*, *PIN*, not *PIN number*). *Large-size soft drink* is redundant because the idea of size is inherent in *large*. See Part III, "Inflated Words," for hundreds of other such redundancies.

references   Keep a record (for yourself and for your bibliography, if you're using one) of every book you consult in the course of your research, along with the page numbers on which you found each bit of information.

When listing references, capitalize all main words in the title and underline or italicize the titles of books, almanacs, catalogs, directories, dictionaries, encyclopedias, handbooks, and manuals.

The simplest format for a book reference in a bibliography is: Strunk, William, Jr., and E.B. White, *The Elements of Style*, 4th ed. (Boston: Allyn and Bacon, 2000). However, almost any arrangement of the identifying elements is acceptable as long as you are consistent throughout the bibliography.

Reserve footnotes for academic or technical writing; in everyday writing you can usually find a way to deliver that information in the text (in the process, you may find it was not necessary). Each footnote is numbered (a superscript in the text, such as [1], and simply *1.* in the footnote). A footnote may consist of a simple sentence of explanation or it may cite a book from which the footnoted material was taken; in that case, use a format like the one above or use one of your own—as long as all elements are included and all citations are treated the same way.

repetition   Repetition can be a vigorous and memorable style choice: "Never trouble trouble till trouble troubles you"; "Don't sell the bear's skin before you have caught the bear"; "Hope is the feeling we have that the feeling we have is not permanent" (Mignon McLaughlin).

Repetition is a problem when writers are unaware of repeating pet words and phrases or of stating the same idea several ways. Conversely, it's a problem when writers are so afraid of repetition that they indulge in "elegant variation," that is, substituting awkward circumlocutions to avoid repeating a word or phrase. For example, in one sentence a woman picks up a cup of coffee. In the next she is sipping "the milky offering" or "the hot liquid."

Roman numerals   A few situations still call for Roman numerals:

1. outlines;
2. parts of a book (this one is divided into Part I, Part II, and Part III, and the front matter pages are numbered i, ii, iii, iv, etc.);
3. names of individuals (Elizabeth I, George Mertoun III) and even wars (World War I);
4. parts of a play (Act II).

run-on sentence   A run-on sentence contains two independent clauses that are linked by a comma instead of by a conjunction. Commas do not link. The following sentence is a run-on: "It's a tough nut to crack, I don't know which way to turn." The two thoughts should be connected by a conjunction ("It's a tough nut to crack, and I don't know which way to turn") or by a semicolon ("It's a tough nut to crack; I don't know which way to turn") or made into two sentences ("It's a tough nut to crack. I don't know which way to turn").

-self   The common error with reflexive pronouns like *myself* is using them instead of the nominative or objective pronoun (*I* or *me*): "As far as my sister and myself are concerned, he has always been a snake in the grass" ("my sister and I" is correct); "The grass is always greener on the other side of the fence for my husband and myself" ("my husband and me" is correct).

Avoid reflexive pronouns such as *myself, yourself, himself, herself* except when

1. the subject and object are the same person or thing: "History repeats itself" ("history repeats history"); "If you want to make a fool of yourself, you'll find a lot of people ready to help you" ("you want to make a fool of you");

2. you want to emphasize a word: "Hunger itself is the best sauce";

3. you want to stress emphasizing that a person did something alone: "She let the cat out of the bag herself."

semicolon The semicolon serves sometimes to connect and sometimes to separate. Use a semicolon to link two sentences with closely related ideas: "Small sorrows speak; great ones are silent"; "They who speak, sow; they who listen, reap." The semicolon provides punch and drama by allowing two related ideas to be closer than they would be with a period between them.

In its other function, the semicolon separates elements that might otherwise confuse the reader: "I remember my father's favorite admonitions: easy come,

easy go; do as I say, not as I do; fish or cut bait; once bit-
ten, twice shy; the bigger they are, the harder they fall."

Because that series contains commas, a semicolon
is needed to separate the phrases from each other. Even if
only one element in the list contains a comma, you must
use a semicolon. The exception is a list of names and ages
("Liz, 31, Katie, 28, Matt, 24, Nora, 23") because there is
no confusion about what goes with what.

sentence   A sentence may have one main idea ("If you
sleep with dogs, you will rise with fleas"), two closely
related ideas ("Feed a cold and starve a fever"), or several ideas or actions ("For want of a nail the shoe was
lost; for want of a shoe the horse was lost; for want of a
horse the rider was lost; for want of a rider the kingdom
was lost").

A sentence may be short ("The die is cast") or long,
but it always has a subject (expressed or implied) and a
verb that together make a complete thought. "Dogs playing" has a subject and a verb form, but it is not a complete
thought. A sentence always ends with a punctuation mark.

In general, the most pleasing sentences contain
from fifteen to thirty words. Introduce longer and shorter
sentences from time to time so that your writing doesn't
become boring.

Vary the type of sentence:

1. A simple sentence consists of one independent
clause (noun plus verb):

"Success breeds confidence" (Beryl Markham).

"Busy people are never busybodies" (Ethel Watts Mumford).

"Dog lovers are a good breed themselves" (Gladys Taber).

"Happiness is nothing but everyday living seen through a veil" (Zora Neale Hurston).

2. A compound sentence consists of two or more independent clauses (or simple sentences) connected by a semicolon, a conjunction, or a word acting as a conjunction:

"There are no old people nowadays; they are either 'wonderful for their age' or dead" (Mary Pettibone Poole).

"A gossip is one who talks to you about others; a bore is one who talks to you about himself; and a brilliant conversationalist is one who talks to you about yourself" (Lisa Kirk).

3. A complex sentence has one independent clause and one or more dependent clauses: "One must never miss an opportunity of quoting things by others, which are always more interesting than those one thinks up one-self" (Marcel Proust).

4. A compound-complex sentence has two or more independent clauses and one or more dependent clauses (see the third sentence):

"I've figured out why first dates don't work any better than they do. It's because they take place in restaurants. Women are weird and confused and unhappy about food, and men are weird and confused and unhappy about money, yet off they go, the minute they meet, to where you use money to buy food" (Adair Lara).

You don't need to know the names of the types of sentences or even how to define them. What you need is to develop an awareness of the different ways you can put words together and to practice using all of them.

The first word of a sentence should not be a number ("13 is a baker's dozen"), nor is it generally a good idea to start sentences with *there is, there are,* or *it is.*

The last words of a sentence contain your most important, most dramatic thought for that sentence.

Play with the various groupings of words, moving them around to see where they look best. Read your sentences out loud—problems tend to stand out.

One of the best things you can do to perfect your sentence-writing ability is to admire and analyze good sentences when you come across them in your reading. See also *run-on sentence, sentence fragment.*

sentence fragment   An incomplete thought followed by a punctuation mark is a sentence fragment: "Books, the children of the brain." "All or nothing!" "When pigs have wings." "Now or never." "No sooner said than done!" Intended sentence fragments can contribute to style when used infrequently and judiciously. Accidental sentence fragments point to a careless writer.

sexist language   See *biased language.*

[**sic**]   Meaning "thus" or "so," [*sic*] tells readers that what they just read wasn't a mistake. Because *sic* is a complete Latin word, there is no period after it; because it is Latin, it is set in italics. It always appears in brackets. Use [*sic*] sparingly because readers can usually figure out what was meant and what was not: "Heads, I win; tails, you lose [*sic*]."

similes   A simile, which compares two unlike things to each other and which is signaled by *like* or *as*, can animate and sharpen your writing by creating images for the reader. The following examples of similes using *as* are familiar—so familiar, in fact, that you should never use them in your writing:

mad as a hornet	old as the hills
strong as an ox	poor as a church mouse
red as a beet	sick as a dog
flat as a pancake	slippery as an eel

The word *like* often signals a more involved simile: "A people without history is like the wind on the buffalo grass"; "Some families are like potatoes; all that is good of them is underground." See also *metaphors.*

slang   Unless you are writing fiction, avoid slang; it tends to diminish your credibility (unless it acts as jargon and actually gives you credibility with a certain audience). When you use it, consider whether it will date your material in a year or two.

slash   The slash, also called a virgule or solidus, has only a few functions: (1) separating alternatives (*and/or*; *compare to/compare with*); (2) standing in for the word *per* ($18/hour); and (3) indicating separate lines of poetry when they are written in prose style: "The human race / Has climbed on protest" (Ella Wheeler Wilcox).

spacing   When you are typing, leave either one or two spaces at the end of a sentence (but be consistent) and one space after all punctuation inside the sentence (except for punctuation followed by another punctuation mark—usually a quotation mark or parenthesis or bracket, in which case you leave no space).

Leave one line of space between paragraphs if you are not indenting.

Do not leave a space between a person's initials, but do leave one between the initials and the last name: L.M. Montgomery.

When submitting writing that will be edited, double-space it (one line of space between each typed line, two lines between paragraphs if you are not indenting).

In all your writing, leave generous margins at top, bottom, and sides to make it easier to read. For letters, leave enough space between the letterhead and the date and between the date and the inside address to make it look attractive on the paper. On the envelope, leave two spaces between the state abbreviation and the Zip + 4 code.

state abbreviations   Most dictionaries list state abbreviations after the state name, beginning with the two-letter code used by the United States Postal Service (CA for California), followed by abbreviations to be used in more formal texts and the inside addresses of letters (Cal. or Calif.).

stereotypes   See *biased language.*

subjunctive   The subjunctive mood of a verb is used today mainly in two broad instances: when something is not real—you are wishing, imagining, supposing (*I wish I were tall, what if he were to die, if only she were here, if he were to arrive early*); and when something is necessary or suggested (*Mother insisted we wear boots, it's important that you unplug it first, they suggested we think it over*).

syllabification   See *word division.*

than I/than me   "My brother likes the dog better than I" means "My brother likes the dog better than I like the dog." "My brother likes the dog better than me" means "My brother likes the dog better than he likes me." The use of *than I* or *than me* depends on whether the pronoun is a subject ("*I* like the dog") or an object ("he likes *me*"). Whenever possible, make your meaning clear (and avoid the wrong usage) by filling in the missing words (the second sentence in each case).

that   The judicious use of the conjunction *that* is an acquired skill. Style and clarity suffer when *that* is not used when it should be—and also when *that* is used when it shouldn't be. The following sentence is smoother with *that* than it would have been without it: "Why is it that when anything goes without saying, it never does?" (Marcelene Cox). Adding *that* after *thing* in the following sentence would have thrown off the rhythm: "It's a good thing there's gravity or else when birds died, they'd stay where they were" (Steven Wright). In some cases, either way is acceptable: "Love is a game that two can play"; "Love is a game two can play." To determine when you need *that*, read your sentence with it and without it to see which sounds better.

that/which   The easiest way to determine whether you want to use *that* or *which* is to see if commas (or sometimes dashes) are appropriate. Commas travel with *which*; they do not accompany *that*. "When elephants fight, it is the grass that suffers." "All is not gold that glitters." "All is well that ends well." You would not have put a comma before *that* in any of those sentences. A second test is to see if you can delete the part that begins with *that* or *which*. If you can delete it without making nonsense of the sentence, you use *which* (and commas). "March, which came in like a lion, went out like a lamb." "If you hunt two hares at once, which is what you appear to be doing, you'll catch neither." "Success doesn't depend on size, which we too often think it does, or a cow would catch a rabbit."

there   Although *there* has its uses, it most often weakens the sentence, especially when it is the first word ("There is . . ."; "There are . . ."). Lucile Vaughan Payne calls *there* "the enemy of style because it seldom adds anything but clutter to a sentence." What word or phrase would you use if there were no such word as *there*?

thing   Only rarely is this the best word for your sentence. Search your writing for *thing* (and *something, anything,* and even *nothing*) to see if you can't replace it with a more descriptive word.

time   Watch for redundancies: it's *noon* and *midnight,* never *12 noon* or *12 midnight;* it's either *six in the morning* or *6 a.m.,* but never *6 a.m. in the morning.* Some publishers set A.M. and P.M. in small capital letters, but unless you are producing text using desktop publishing software, type them lowercase. Don't capitalize seasons or time periods (*week, month*), but do capitalize months and days of the week. Centuries are generally spelled out (*fourteenth century*); A.D. and B.C. are typed as capitals (except, again, for publishers, who set them in small caps); and decades can be written in several ways: *1920s, mid-1980s, the '50s, the Gay Nineties, the late '60s, the forties.*

titles   When typing, use italics for titles of books, movies, plays, operas, magazines, newspapers, paintings, drawings, and statues (unless you're writing for a publication that handles titles some other way). For newspapers, city names are added and italicized: *Minneapolis Star Tribune*, not Minneapolis *Star Tribune* (generally omit *The*). If your e-mail doesn't have an italic font, set off normally italicized titles with asterisks: "Have you read *Tempest in a Teapot*?"

The names of smaller works—poems, articles, essays, short stories, TV series, song titles—are set in regular type with quotation marks ("Going to the Dogs").

Capitalize all words of a title except *a, an, the, and, but, for, nor, or,* and prepositions of three or fewer letters (*in, of, to*). These words are capitalized, however, if they are the first or last words in the title. See also *italics, quotation marks.*

tone   The tone you choose for your writing depends on your content (is your material academic, humorous, informational?) and on your audience (will you reach them best with a conversational tone, a forceful tone, or an emotional tone?). Among hundreds of tones, writing can appear preachy, genial, stilted, relaxed, formal, informal, light, serious, pedantic, sarcastic, angry, boastful, timid, unsure, mysterious, or lewd. If you don't consciously choose and fashion your tone, your writing will still have a tone, but it may not be what you intended. Whatever tone you choose, maintain it throughout the piece.

too   At the end of a clause you don't need a comma before *too* ("You can't have your cake and eat it too"). Elsewhere in a sentence, set off *too* by commas ("I, too, have many irons in the fire").

trademarks and trade names   A trademark (identified by TM next to the name) means that that term is legally restricted to the company that owns it. A trade name, or brand name, may or may not be registered as a trademark. The dictionary identifies some words that are trademarked (*Band-Aid, Caterpillar, Xerox*); capitalize these words when you use them. When appropriate, insert the ™ and describe the item generically ("Kleenex™ paper tissue").

transitions   Transitional words and phrases take you from one idea to the next, from one sentence to the next, from one paragraph to the next, and even from one part of the sentence or paragraph to another part. Lead readers logically from thought to thought with words like these:

as a result	in the meantime
at the same time	in the same way
because of	later
consequently	similarly
for example	subsequently
in/by contrast	therefore
in addition	thus

try to   Careful writers will avoid the ungrammatical *try and*, which is sometimes heard in informal speech.

underlining   When writing in longhand or using a typewriter, underline words that should be in italics.

verbs   In the matter of style, verbs are one of the most rewarding places to invest your energy and creativity. By their verbs shall you know them (the good writers, that is). Learn to tell a strong verb from a weak one; in particular, try to upgrade forms of the verb *to be* (*is, am, was, were, being, been, will be*) to verbs with more action, originality, and color. So-called helping verbs (particularly *to be* and *to have*) just clog the pipes. In 1872, George Eliot wrote of some other helping verbs, "Might, could, would—they are contemptible auxiliaries." Many decades later, people say "could've, would've, should've" to refer to the might-have-beens of the wishy-washy.

Beware of "You could *of* heard a pin drop" instead of "You could *have* heard a pin drop."

In addition to noticing the effective verb choices of your favorite writers, make a notebook or computer file list of verbs that appeal to you. The more good verbs you are familiar with, the more choices you'll have, and the better your chances of finding the right one for your sentence.

very   Reread your writing and cut out every *very* that you can. Then go back and cut out the rest. Consider the strength of these sentences without *very*: Death is a [very] great leveler. Time is the [very] best medicine. The [very] rich never lack relatives. [Very] Few words are best.

voice, active and passive   Active voice means someone or something is doing something ("The worm turns"). Passive voice means someone or something is being done unto ("The barrel was spoiled by one rotten apple"). In almost all cases use the active voice. (That sentence is in the active voice.) The passive voice should be saved for special situations. (That sentence is in the passive voice.)

The active voice is dynamic, direct, and vivid; it supplies the action that moves your piece along. Use the passive voice when you want to emphasize what's being done, rather than who's doing it ("The house was destroyed by last year's freak tornado"). Use it when you need to be tactful or to avoid assigning blame ("The cart was put before the horse in the Lilley case").

while   In addition to its original meaning of *at the same time* or *during the time that* ("Strike while the iron is hot"), *while* has come to be used in place of *whereas*, *although*, and *but* ("Some people eat to live, while others live to eat"). Watch for ambiguity, when *while* may mean either *at the same time* or *although*: "While the mills of the gods grind slowly, they grind exceedingly fine."

When you mean *and*, use it instead of *while*: "Cynics know the price of everything while they know the value of nothing" should be "Cynics know the price of everything and the value of nothing."

who/whom/whoever/whomever   *Who* and *whoever* are subjects: "Who put a spoke in my wheel?" "Whoever loves me, loves my dog."

Whom and *whomever* are objects: "It is human nature to hate those whom we have injured" (Tacitus). "You always get on your high horse with whomever I bring home." *Whomever* is graceless even when used correctly. Used incorrectly in an attempt to sound more refined, it is an embarrassment: "Please mail this file to whomever is elected secretary." *Whoever* is the correct form; it is the subject of the clause ("the person who is elected secretary"). Unless you have a good grasp of it, consider shelving *whomever* permanently.

Who and its related forms refer only to people, not to animals, things, or ideas.

who's/whose   Do you mean to say "who is"? If you do, you want *who's* ("The person who's paying the piper calls the tune"). To show ownership use *whose* ("Whose bull is in the china shop?"). Incidentally, *who* is used only for people, whereas *whose* can refer to ownership by people, animals, or things.

-wise   This clunky suffix is better avoided except for the legitimate *clockwise*, *likewise*, and *otherwise* ("Some are wise and some are otherwise"). The overuse of *-wise* has made it an object of parody: "As a lifelong fashion dropout, I have still read enough fashion mags while waiting at the dentist's to know that the object of fashion is to make A Statement—all I've achieved, statement-wise, is 'Woman Who Wears Clothes So She Won't Be Naked'" (Molly Ivins).

word division   The dictionary shows how words are divided into syllables. You may not need to be overly concerned about syllabification: word-processing software provides automatic word division at the end of a line (although these can be awkward), and editors or printers will double-check hyphenation of material to be published.

word order   You may have all the right words, but some may be in the wrong order. Move your words and phrases around until you achieve clarity and harmony. The following ideas could have been shaped several ways:

> "As to the adjective: when in doubt, strike it out" (Mark Twain).
>
> "Britt ate lots of chocolate but never got fat—a sure sign of demonic possession" (Erica Jong).
>
> "Learning too soon our limitations, we never learn our powers" (Mignon McLaughlin).
>
> "People who want to share their religious views with you almost never want you to share yours with them" (Dave Barry).

words/letters used as words/letters   Use either italics or quotation marks to set apart words or letters you're discussing as words or letters: "Ifs" and "buts" butter no bread/*Ifs* and *buts* butter no bread. Single words and letters tend to look better in italics; longer phrases look bet-

ter in quotation marks. Whichever you choose, be consistent and keep this usage to a minimum. Too many quotation marks on a page look like hiccups, and too much
italic type makes the text appear unnecessarily technical.

zero   Avoid a chain of zeros. Write "$12 million" instead
of "$12,000,000."

Part III

Troublesome Words and Phrases

Writing teaches writing. Your writing will teach you how to write if you work hard enough and have enough faith.

—BONNIE FRIEDMAN

Misspelled

Learn to recognize words with tricky spellings and to look them up in the dictionary. Commonly misspelled words include:

abscess

absence

accommodate

accumulate

acknowledge/
    acknowledgment/
    acknowledging

acquaintance

acquisition

ad nauseam

all right (never "alright")

allotted

a lot (never "alot")

amateur

appall/appalled/appalling

apparatus

aquarium

arctic

auxiliary

beneficiary

benefited

boundary

canceled/cancellation

Caribbean

category

cemetery

chaise longue

commitment

concur/concurred/concurrence

consensus

consistency

correspondence/correspondent

daylight-saving time

desperate

discernible

ecstasy

eligible

embarrass/embarrassment

exhilarate

existence

February

first come, first served

fluorescence

foreign

fulfill/fulfilled/fulfillment

genealogy

grievance

guerrilla

harass/harassment

height (never "heighth")

hemorrhage

hitchhike/hitchhiker

hypocrisy

impostor

indispensable

in regard to

inoculate

iridescent/iridescence

irresistible

jewel/jeweled/jeweler/
  jewelry

judgment

knowledgeable

liaison

lieutenant

maintenance

maneuver

Mediterranean

miniature

minuscule

mischievous

missile

misspell

necessary

neighbor

niece

noticeable

occasion

occur/occurred/
  occurrence

omitted

ophthalmology

parallel

paraphernalia

pastime

perennial

permissible

perseverance

personnel

precede

prejudice

privilege

proceed

Realtor

receive

recur/recurrence

refrigerator

regardless (never
  "irregardless")

roommate

sacrilegious

seize

siege

sieve

subtle

threshold

toward

until or till
   (never "'til")

vengeance

Confused

When using one of the following words, check its definition in the dictionary. Starred words are discussed in Part II: A–Z Style Guide.

accept/except

adapt/adept/adopt

advice/advise

affect/effect

alleged/accused

all ready/already

allude/refer

allusion/illusion

alternate/alternative

altogether/all together

*amount/number

anxious/eager

*as/like

assure/ensure/insure

attorney/lawyer

authentic/genuine

average/mean/medium/
   norm

*awhile/a while

*bad/badly

beside/besides

*between/among

*bi-/semi-

boat/ship

born/borne

bring/take

burned/burnt

*can/may

capital/capitol

cite/sight/site

common/mutual

*compare to/compare
  with

compare/contrast

complement/compliment

*compose/comprise

consul/council/counsel

continual/continuous

*convince/persuade

credible/creditable

criteria/criterion

definite/definitive

*different from/
  different than

disinterested/uninterested

disorganized/unorganized

*each other/one another

emigrate/immigrate

eminent/immanent/
  imminent

envious/jealous

*farther/further

*fewer/less

*flammable/inflammable

flaunt/flout

foreword/forward

formally/formerly

*good/well

healthful/healthy

*imply/infer

in behalf/on behalf

ingenious/ingenuous

*its/it's

*lay/lie

liqueur/liquor

may/might

*me/myself

meantime/meanwhile

militate/mitigate

must/should

oral/verbal

phenomena/phenomenon

pore/pour

principal/principle

prophecy/prophesy

reaction/response

Scot/Scotch/Scottish

set/sit

stationary/stationery

*than I/than me

*that/which

their/there/they're

United Kingdom/
    England/Britain or
    Great Britain

*who/whom/whoever/
    whomever

*who's/whose

your/you're

Inflated

Replace the overblown terms on the left with those on the right. (In a few contexts, the word or phrase on the left may be what you want.)

absolutely essential/absolutely necessary/absolutely complete = essential/necessary/complete

accompanied by = with

accordingly = so

according to our records = we find, our records show (or omit)

acknowledge receipt of = thank you for

acquaint = tell, inform, let know

acquire = get, gain

activate = begin, start

active consideration = consideration

actual experience/actual truth/actual facts = experience/
truth/facts

actually authentic = authentic

added increments = increments

add up = add

adequate enough = adequate or enough (not both)

advance forward = advance

advance planning/advance preparation/advance warning
= planning/preparation/warning

advance reservations = reservations

advise = tell, inform

affix your signature = sign your name

afford an opportunity = allow, permit

after the conclusion of = after

aggregate/aggregation = total

a great deal of = much

all and sundry = all

all of = all

all throughout = throughout

all-time record = record

almost similar = similar

along the lines of = like

already exists = exists

a majority of = most

and etc. = etc.

and so on and so forth = and so on

an early date = soon

anent = about, concerning

another additional = another

anticipate = expect

a number of = about

a number of cases = some, several

any and all = any or all (not both)

applicable to = suitable for, relevant, appropriate

appreciate = realize

appreciate in value = appreciate

appreciate your informing me = please write, tell me

approximately = about

are in receipt of = have received

are of the opinion that = think that

around about [number] = about [number]

ascertain = learn, find out

as far as I am concerned = as for me

as for example = for example

ask the question = ask

as of this date = today

as per = according to

as per your request = as you requested

as regards = concerning, about

assemble together = assemble

assist/assistance = help

as to = about (or omit)

at about = at

at all times = always

at an early date/at a later date (or time) = soon/later

at a time when = when

ATM machine = ATM or automated teller machine

at present = now

attached please find/attached herewith/attached hereto = attached, I am attaching, I am enclosing

attach together = attach

at that point in time/at this point in time = then/now

at the conclusion of = after

at the earliest possible moment = immediately, very soon

at the moment = now, just now

at the present time/at this writing = now

at your earliest convenience = soon

awaiting your instructions = please let me know

baby puppies = puppies

balance of equilibrium = balance or equilibrium (not both)

based on the fact that = because

basic fundamentals/basic essentials = fundamentals/ essentials

beat up = beat

be cognizant of = know that

be dependent on = depend on

be in possession of = possess

be the recipient of = receive

beyond a shadow of a doubt = undoubtedly

big in size = big

bona fide = genuine

both agree = agree

both alike = alike or both

both tied for second place = tied for second place

brief moment = moment

but at the same time = but or at the same time (not both)

but even so = but or even so (not both)

but however/but nevertheless/but nonetheless = one word or the other, but not both

but in any case = but or in any case (not both)

but on the other hand = but or on the other hand (not both)

by means of = by, with

call your attention to = please note

cancel out = cancel

caucus meeting = caucus or meeting (not both)

cease = stop

circa = about

circle around = circle

classify into groups = classify

close proximity = proximity, nearby, close by

close up = close

co-equal = equal

cognizant = aware

collaborate together = collaborate

combine together = combine

come to the realization = realize

commence = begin, start

commendation = praise

common accord = accord

communicate = write, telephone

communication = letter, call, message

commute back and forth = commute

complete and unabridged = complete or unabridged
(not both)

completely fill/completely finish = fill/finish

completely accurate/completely compatible/completely exhausted/completely finished/completely unanimous = accurate/compatible/exhausted/finished/unanimous

complete monopoly/complete stop = monopoly/stop

conclude = close, end

conclusion = closing

conclusive proof = proof

consensus of opinion = consensus

construct = make

continue on = continue

continue to remain = remain

cooperate together = cooperate

cover over = cover

critical/crucial = important

current news = news

customary channels = usual way, regular procedure

customary practice = practice

cylindrical in shape = cylindrical

dead carcass = carcass

decline = turn down, refuse

deeds and actions = deeds or actions (not both)

deem = consider, think

deem it advisable = suggest

definite decision = decision

demonstrate = show

depreciate in value = depreciate

deserving of = deserve

desire = want

despite the fact that = although

direct confrontation = confrontation

discontinue = stop

disincentive – penalty

distance of ten yards/distance of six feet = ten yards/ six feet

doctorate degree = doctorate

do not hesitate to = please

drop down = drop

due consideration = consideration

due to the fact that = because

during the course of = during

during the time that = while

each and every = each or every (not both)

eat up = eat

effectuate = effect

either one of the two = either one, either of the two, either

eliminate = get rid of

emotional feelings = feelings

empty space = space

enclosed herewith/enclosed please find = enclosed,
I enclose

encounter = meet

endeavor = try

endeavor to ascertain = try to find out

endorse on the back = endorse

end result = result

engineer by profession = engineer

entirely destroyed = destroyed

equally as = equally

equivalent = equal

etc. = (avoid when possible)

eventual outcome = outcome

eventuate = result

exactly identical = identical

exactly the same = the same

exact replica = replica

exact same = exact or same (not both)

exhibits the ability to = can

existing condition = condition

expedite = hurry

extreme hazard = hazard

facilitate = ease, simplify, chair the meeting

fact of the matter = fact

false illusion = illusion

fearful of = fear

feedback = comments, advice, reactions, opinions, thoughts

feel free to call/feel free to write = please call/please write

fellow colleague = colleague

few and far between = few

few in number = few

field of anthropology/field of politics = anthropology/politics

filled to capacity = filled

filthy dirty = filthy or dirty (not both)

final conclusion/final outcome = conclusion/outcome

finalize = end, conclude, complete, settle

find necessary = need

finish up = finish

first and foremost = first or foremost (not both)

first begin/first create/first discover/first originate = begin/create/discover/originate

first of all = first

flat plateau = plateau

fold up = fold

foot pedal = pedal

foreign imports = imports

formulate = form

for the period of a week/month/year = for a week/
    month/year

for the purpose of = for

for the reason that = because, since, as, for

forthwith = now, at once

free gift = gift

fullest possible extent = fully

full satisfaction = satisfaction

fully intact = intact

furnish = give

future plan/future prospects = plan/prospects

gather together = gather

general consensus = consensus

give an answer = answer

give encouragement to = encourage

good benefit = benefit

grand total = total

grateful thanks = thanks

great majority = majority

grind up = grind

hastily improvised = improvised

have a belief in = believe

have a tendency to = tend to

head up = head

heir apparent = heir

helpful cooperation = cooperation

hence = so

herein = in this

hereinafter = from now on

herewith = enclosed, attached

hired mercenary = mercenary

homologous = alike

hopeful optimism = optimism

hopefully = we hope, it is to be hoped

hopeful that = hope

hurry up = hurry

if and when = if or when (not both)

if at all possible = if possible

if it meets with your approval = if you approve

if you desire = if you wish, if you want

immediately adjoining = adjoining

immediately following = then

implement = carry out, do, put into effect

I myself personally = I or I myself

in about a week's time = in a week

in accordance with = with, as, by, under

in addition, they also = in addition or also (not both)

in addition to = besides

inadvertent oversight = oversight

in a matter of seconds/minutes/hours/days = in seconds/
    minutes/hours/days

in a number of cases = sometimes, some

in a place where = where

in a satisfactory manner = satisfactorily

inasmuch as = as, since, because

inaugurate = begin, start

in back of = behind

in close proximity = near

in common with each other = in common

in compliance with your request = as you requested,
    as you asked

in connection with = about, in, on, to (or omit)

increase by a factor of two = double

indicate = show

individual person = individual or person (not both)

inform = tell

initial = first

initiate = begin, start

in lieu of = instead of

in many cases = often

in order that = so that

in order to = to

input = advice, opinions, thoughts, reactions

inquire = ask

in re = about

in receipt of = received

in reference to/in regard to = about, concerning

inside of = inside

integral part = part

interface with – meet with

in the amount of = for

in the course of = during

in the event of/in the event that = if

in the form of = as

in the immediate vicinity of = near

in the majority of instances = usually, often

in the meantime = meanwhile

in the nature of = like

in the near future = soon

in the neighborhood of = about

in the possession of = has, have

in the time of = during

in the vast majority of cases = in most cases

in this day and age = today (or omit)

in view of = because, since

in view of the fact that = as

invisible to the eye = invisible

invited guest = guest

I share your concern = like you, I believe

is indicative of = indicates

is located in = is in

is of the opinion = thinks

it has been brought to our notice = we note, we have learned

it is clear/it is obvious = clearly/obviously

it is my intention = I intend

it would not be unreasonable to believe/think/assume = I believe/think/assume

I would hope = I hope

I would like to express my appreciation = I appreciate

Jewish rabbi = rabbi

joint collaboration = collaboration

join together = join

just exactly = exactly

keep in mind the fact that = remember that

kindly = please

kneel down = kneel

last but not least = finally (or omit)

lift up = lift

likewise = and, also

little baby = baby

look back in retrospect = look back

lose out = lose

major breakthrough = breakthrough

make a decision = decide

make a mention of = mention

make inquiry regarding = inquire about

make reference to = refer to

mandatory requirements = requirements

may perhaps = may

meaningless gibberish = gibberish

meet with approval = approve

meet together = meet

meet up with = meet

mental telepathy = telepathy

merge together = merge

modification = change

modus operandi = method

month of December = December

more preferable = preferable

multitude of people = multitude

mutual agreement/mutual cooperation = agreement/
  cooperation

my personal opinion = my opinion, I believe that

native habitat = habitat

natural instinct = instinct

necessary prerequisite = prerequisite

never before = never

new initiative/new innovation/new record/new recruit =
  initiative/innovation/record/recruit

none at all = none

not in a position to = unable to

notwithstanding the fact that = although, even though

obviate = do away with

official business = business

off of = off

of the opinion that = think, believe

old adage = adage

on a continuing basis = constantly, continually

on a daily/monthly/weekly basis = daily/monthly/weekly

on a few occasions = occasionally

on a regular basis = regularly

on a theoretical basis = theoretically

on behalf of = for

one and the same = the same

only other alternative = alternative

on the grounds that = because, since

on the order of = about

on the part of = by, for, among

opening gambit = gambit

original founder/original source = founder/source

other alternative = alternative

outdoor patio = patio

outside of = outside

overexaggerate = exaggerate

over with = over

owing to/owing to the fact that = because of

owing to unforeseen circumstances = unexpectedly

pack up = pack

particulars = details

past experience/past history/past memories =
     experience/history/memories

peace and quiet = peace or quiet (not both)

per = a

per annum = a year

per diem = a day

perfectly clear = clear

perform an examination = examine

permeate throughout = permeate

per se = as such

personal friend/personal opinion/personal belief = friend/opinion/belief

peruse = study

pervasive = widespread

pervasively = throughout

pick and choose = pick or choose (not both)

place emphasis on = emphasize

polish up = polish

positive identification = identification

postponed until later = postponed

predicated on = based on

preparatory to = before

prepared to offer = able to offer

preplanned = planned

present a conclusion = conclude

present here = present or here (not both)

present incumbent/present status = incumbent/status

preventative/orientated = preventive/oriented

previous experience = experience

previous to = before

prioritize = list, rank, rate

prior to = before

pure unadulterated = pure or unadulterated (not both)

pursuant to = according to

quantify = measure

quite unique = unique

radically new = new or radical (not both)

raise up = raise

raison d'être = reason for

rarely ever/seldom ever = rarely/seldom

raze to the ground = raze

reach an agreement = agree

rectangular in shape = rectangular

reduce to a minimum = minimize

red in color/yellow in color/blue in color = red/
    yellow/blue

refer back = refer

regarding = about

regular routine = routine

reiterate again = reiterate

relating to/relative to = about, concerning

remuneration = pay

repeat again = repeat

reside = live

return back/retreat back/revert back = return/retreat/
    revert

rise up = rise

root cause = cause

round circles = round or circles (not both)

round in shape = round

same ("will send same") = it, them, the items (or omit)

same identical = same or identical (not both)

seldom ever = seldom

separate entities = entities

serious crisis/serious danger = crisis/danger

set a new record = set a record

settle up = settle

shuttle back and forth = shuttle

similar to = like

simple reason = reason

sine qua non = essential

sink down = sink

six in number = six

slow down/slow up = slow

small in size = small

small village = village

so advise us = advise us

so as to be able to = to

so consequently = so or consequently (not both)

so therefore = so or therefore (not both)

spell out = spell

spoken dialogue = dialogue

spring up = spring

square in shape = square

stand up = stand

state of Minnesota = Minnesota

strangled to death = strangled

streamlined in appearance = streamlined

still persists/still remains = persists/remains

straighten up = straighten

string together = string

subject matter = subject or matter (not both)

subsequent to = after, following

substantiate = prove

successful achievement = achievement

sudden impulse/sudden collapse/sudden crisis = impulse/collapse/crisis

sufficient = enough

sum total = total

sweep up = sweep

sworn affidavit/sworn oath = affidavit/oath

technical jargon = jargon

temporary truce = truce

terminate = end, complete, finish, conclude

the better part of = most of, nearly all of

the bulk of = most of, nearly all of

the earliest possible moment = soon, immediately

therein = in

the undersigned/this writer = I

this is to thank you = thank you

thusly = in this way, as follows

tiny inkling = inkling

together with = with

too numerous to mention = numerous

total destruction = destruction

totally wrong = wrong

transmit = send

true fact = fact

tuna fish = tuna

two opposites = opposites

ubiquitous = widespread

ultimate outcome = outcome

undergraduate student = undergraduate

under separate cover = separately

unexpected emergency/unexpected surprise =
emergency/surprise

uniformly homogeneous = homogeneous

unintentional mistake = mistake

universal panacea = panacea

unless and until = unless or until (not both)

until such time as = until

untimely death = death

up to this writing = until now

urban cities = cities

usual custom/usual habit = custom/habit

utilization/utilize = use

vacillating back and forth = vacillating

various different = various or different (not both)

verbal discussion = discussion

visible to the eye = visible

vitally essential = vital or essential (not both)

wake up = wake

wall mural = mural

whether or not = whether

wide expanse = expanse

wind up = wind

wish to apologize = we apologize

with a view to = to

without further delay = now, immediately

with reference to/with regard to/with respect to = about, concerning (or omit)

with the exception of = except for

with the result that = so that

with this in mind, it is certainly clear that = therefore

worthy of merit = worthy or merits (not both)

would appreciate your informing us/would appreciate your advising us = let us know

writer by profession = writer

Unnecessary

Strengthen your writing by deleting words and phrases such as those listed below. The worst offenders are *very*, *really*, *so*, *quite*, and *rather*.

above-mentioned	apparently
absolutely	as a matter of fact
aforementioned	as a rule
almost	as a usual case
also	as I am sure you know
although	as the case may be
always	as to whether

as you know

at hand

beg to [state/differ/advise]

besides

be that as it may

commonly

dare say

different [as in two
different dresses, sev-
eral different movies]

duly

essentially

even

for all intents and purposes

for my part

frankly

generally

give this matter your
attention

honestly

I believe

I feel

I think

in all honesty

in general

in many instances

in most cases

in my judgment

in my opinion

in the final analysis

in this connection

intrinsically

it goes without saying

it is possible that

it seems/it appears

just

kind of

literally

literally and figuratively

lot/lots/a whole lot

maybe

more or less

mostly

needless to say

normally

not to mention

often

ordinarily

overall

perhaps

permit me to say

personally

quite/quite a

rather

really

respectively

seemingly

seems to indicate

so

sometimes

somewhat

sort of

such

take and (for example,
    "take and read this")

take the liberty of/take
    this opportunity to

the above

there is a possibility that

there is some potential
    that

this is to inform you

to me

to tell the truth

too

totally

type of

unless

usually

very

we are writing to tell you

well and good

when all is said and done/
    after all is said and
    done

wish to advise/wish to
    state

with all due regard

words cannot describe

Index